Designing Butterfly Exhibits

Nicole Sipe

Smithsonian

Contributing Author

Heather Schultz, M.A.

Consultants

Cindy Brown
Supervisory Horticulturalist
Collections Specialist
Smithsonian Gardens

Gary Krupnick, Ph.D.
Head of the Plant Conservation Unit
Department of Botany, National
Museum of Natural History

Tamieka Grizzle, Ed.D.
K–5 STEM Lab Instructor
Harmony Leland Elementary School

Stephanie Anastasopoulos, M.Ed.
TOSA, STREAM Integration
Solana Beach School District

Publishing Credits

Rachelle Cracchiolo, M.S.Ed., *Publisher*
Conni Medina, M.A.Ed., *Managing Editor*
Diana Kenney, M.A.Ed., NBCT, *Series Developer*
June Kikuchi, *Content Director*
Véronique Bos, *Creative Director*
Robin Erickson, *Art Director*
Seth Rogers, *Editor*
Mindy Duits, *Senior Graphic Designer*
Smithsonian Science Education Center

Image Credits: back cover, p.5 (top), p.11 (bottom), p.12, p.13 (bottom), p.18 (all), p.19 © Smithsonian; p.6 (right), p.7 (bottom), p.16 (right) Gregory G. Dimijian/Science Source; p.7 (top) Francesco Tomasinelli/Science Source; pp.10–11 Chris Jenner/Shutterstock; p.13 (top) GFC Collection/NHPA/Photoshot/Newscom; p.15 (bottom) Simon Fraser/Science Source; p.16 Per-Anders Pettersson/Getty Images; p.18, p.20 Robin Chittenden/Alamy; p.19 (top), p.21 (top) Oli Scarff/Getty Images; p.19 (bottom right), 21 (bottom right) Will & Deni McIntyre/Science Source; p.19 (bottom left), p.21 (bottom left) Louise Murray/Science Source; p.22 (left) Susan Biddle/The Washington Post/Getty Images; p.25 (bottom) B.G. Thomson/Science Source; all other images from iStock and/or Shutterstock.

Library of Congress Cataloging-in-Publication Data

Names: Sipe, Nicole, author.
Title: Designing butterfly exhibits / Nicole Sipe.
Description: Huntington Beach, CA : Teacher Created Materials, [2019] | Audience: Grade 4 to 6. | Includes index. |
Identifiers: LCCN 2018005201 (print) | LCCN 2018015918 (ebook) | ISBN 9781493869312 (E-book) | ISBN 9781493866915 (paperback)
Subjects: LCSH: Butterflies--Exhibitions--Juvenile literature.
Classification: LCC QL545.2 (ebook) | LCC QL545.2 .S57 2019 (print) | DDC 595.78/9074--dc23
LC record available at https://lccn.loc.gov/2018005201

Smithsonian

Teacher Created Materials

5301 Oceanus Drive
Huntington Beach, CA 92649-1030
www.tcmpub.com

ISBN 978-1-4938-6691-5

Printed by 51250
PO 10851 / Printed in USA

Table of Contents

Beautiful Butterflies

A brightly colored butterfly spreads its wings and takes flight. A spotted butterfly drinks sweet nectar from a nearby flower. A group of butterflies flutters around a flowering bush, looking for places to land.

From where you stand, you see butterflies flit and float around you. Their delicate wings brush against your arms. They dance in front of your eyes. You are surrounded by winged creatures. Lush plants and blooming flowers are everywhere in this warm and **humid** (HYOO-mid) place.

A place where you can go and be surrounded by butterflies might seem like a dream. But butterfly exhibits are real. They serve an important role, too.

Butterflies are an important part of **ecosystems**. Sadly, many butterfly species are at risk of **extinction**. This is where butterfly exhibits come in. In enclosed spaces, we can learn more about these winged creatures. We can see how their lives are linked with the plants they depend on. And, we can learn what we can do to protect these insects from the dangers of living in the wild.

A group of butterflies is called a kaleidoscope (kuh-LIE-duh-skohp). A group of caterpillars is called an army.

tree nymph butterfly

In the Wild

Butterflies are more than just bright colors and pretty wings. They help to **pollinate** flowers and plants. Many plants depend on pollinators, such as butterflies, to survive. Without them, these plants would not be able to grow new seeds.

Butterflies are also important to food chains. They are food for other animals. Many birds, bats, and mice eat butterflies and caterpillars. When butterflies leave or die, the animals that eat them have less food. They will soon move to a new place that has more food for them. In turn, larger animals that eat birds, bats, and mice have less to eat, too.

Scientists use butterflies to measure the health of an area. If butterflies leave a place or begin to die in large numbers, scientists pay attention. It is a sign that something has changed. More problems may be on the way. The opposite is true, too. Seeing lots of butterflies and caterpillars is a good sign that an area is healthy.

A bird catches a caterpillar.

A mouse feeds on monarch butterflies.

A praying mantis eats a butterfly.

Butterflies pollinate more plants than any other insect except for bees.

A butterfly collects pollen from a plant.

Life in the wild is hard for butterflies. In the last 20 years, the population of many types of wild butterflies has dropped. This is especially true for the monarch butterfly.

In the 1990s, there were more than 1 billion monarchs in the world. Over the next 25 years, that number dropped to 35 million. No one knows for sure why this happened. But scientists have a few ideas.

Some scientists think butterflies are laying fewer eggs than they did in the past. **Herbicides** (UHR-buh-sides) are sprayed on big areas of land to kill weeds. The sprays also kill the plants that butterflies feed from and lay eggs on. This is a big problem. Butterflies fill many roles in their ecosystems. Without them, many things go undone.

A butterfly lays eggs.

A worker sprays herbicides.

Monarch butterflies land on tree branches.

MATHEMATICS

Counting on Butterflies

Scientists keep track of how many butterflies live in the wild. But counting each one would take too long. Instead, scientists estimate. They count small groups of butterflies. Sometimes, they see butterflies in very large groups, or clusters. In these cases, they count a small section and use that number to estimate how many there are in the cluster.

Learning Takes Flight

The numbers do not lie. Butterflies are dying off. Scientists have known about this for many years. And yet, there are many people who still do not know about this problem. Scientists want to spread the word. The more people there are who know about problems that butterflies face, the more people there will be to help find solutions.

One solution is to build more butterfly exhibits. These spaces offer hands-on learning. Visitors can use all of their senses to learn about butterflies and their **habitats**.

Butterfly exhibits are set up so people can see butterflies in action. Most people have only seen these insects fly, feed, or rest. But butterflies do a lot more! Exhibits are places where people can learn about butterfly behaviors up close.

A butterfly lands on a child's hand.

Some butterflies have short lifespans, so farmers regularly ship butterflies to exhibits.

The Design Process

Butterfly exhibits can be found all over the world. They are great places to see butterflies up close. In these spaces, you can see butterflies act as they would in the wild. You might even see caterpillars or **pupas** (PYOO-puhs) on display.

Every detail in a butterfly exhibit is carefully thought out long before insects and plants are brought in. Each exhibit must be a safe space where butterflies can **thrive**. Designers use what they know about butterflies in the wild to help them build the exhibits.

Designing starts with the room that will be used. Some rooms are much better for butterfly exhibits than others. For example, exhibits often have lots of windows. This is because butterflies love sunlight. They need it to live. Windows bring in light from outside. Special lights can be added to give butterflies even more heat and light.

pupas on display at an exhibit

The glass walls at the Dancing Wings Butterfly Garden in New York let sunlight in.

ARTS

Living Art

Butterflies have inspired artists for thousands of years. Drawings of butterflies have even been found in caves! Some artists like butterflies' bright colors and the way they look as they float through the air. Others are interested in their **compelling** life cycles. Many cultures have linked butterflies to the human soul. In fact, the ancient Greek word for "soul," *psyche* (SIGH-kee), was also used for butterfly.

butterflies in Korean art

Plant Plans

Once a room is designed, the rest of the habitat is created. Choosing plants is a big part of this. Plants are an important part of every butterfly habitat. Butterflies need different plants for many reasons. Each plant in an exhibit must be chosen carefully.

First and foremost, plants are a butterfly's food source. But not every butterfly likes to eat the same type of food. Some butterflies feed on the nectar in flowers. Bee balm and lavender are two types of flowers that have nectar. Other butterflies prefer to feed on juice from ripe fruit. Trays of cut oranges, melons, or plums are common sights at an exhibit.

Plants also play a role in butterfly **breeding**. In the wild, butterflies are picky about where they lay their eggs. They pick plants, such as milkweed, with leaves that will be a good food source for their young once they hatch. A butterfly will not lay eggs if the right kinds of plants are not present. If an exhibit wants to breed butterflies, they need to know which plants to include.

A monarch butterfly feeds on milkweed.

Butterflies taste with their feet. They have sensors on their feet that are similar to the taste buds on your tongue.

Butterlies eat from a tray of oranges and watermelon.

A red admiral butterfly feeds on a lilac bush.

The Heat Is On

Finally, the perfect **climate** must be chosen. Butterfly exhibits are hot and humid. The temperature is kept around 27° Celsius (80° Fahrenheit). There is a high level of humidity. You can feel the moisture in the air. Exhibits are kept this way for a reason. Butterflies are cold-blooded. They need to be warm to fly. When it is too cool, they cannot move. Warm butterflies are more active.

Butterfly Farms

Once a habitat has been designed and built, it is ready for butterflies. Hundreds of butterflies can live in an exhibit at one time. Where do scientists get so many butterflies? They do not walk around with giant nets and capture them in the wild! Instead, they rely on butterfly farms.

Most butterfly farms are in places where a lot of butterflies already live. They include Mexico, South America, and Africa. Farmers in these areas raise adult butterflies. They care for them so that they will breed. After butterflies lay their eggs, farmers collect the eggs by hand.

A woman tends to her butterfly farm.

This wooden structure holds many pupas at a butterfly farm.

SCIENCE

Make It Hot

Butterflies cannot fly if it is colder than 12°C (55°F). This is because their wings absorb heat from the sun. The heat helps them move around. They also love bright sunshine. Exhibits have to bring this ideal setting indoors to keep butterflies happy and healthy.

From Egg to Butterfly

When butterfly eggs hatch, caterpillars come out! Caterpillars eat a lot. Some can eat 27,000 times their own body weights! All this food helps them grow. They grow quickly and shed their skin about four times. Then, it is time for the pupa stage. Caterpillars form shells around themselves. The shell is called a **chrysalis** (KRIH-suh-liss). Once these shells have formed, they are ready to be sent to an exhibit. Pupas can be shipped all around the world.

When scientists at exhibits get pupas, they carefully pin them to boards. Then, they wait. Soon, butterflies come out. Now, the butterflies are ready to fly around their new homes!

Butterfly farms are good for butterfly exhibits. But they also help protect butterflies in the wild. Wild butterfly habitats are disappearing all over the world. Forests where they live and breed are being chopped down. Homes are being built in the fields where they once lived. Chemicals are being sprayed on the plants they eat. But butterfly farmers use land for the good of butterflies.

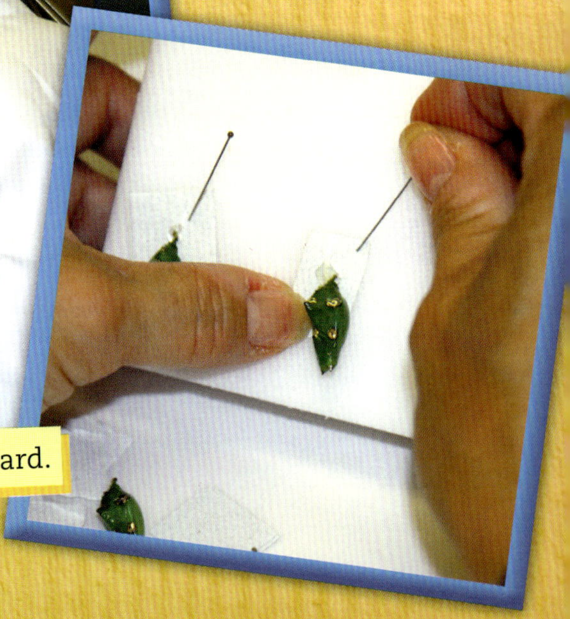

Pupas are attached to a board.

ENGINEERING

Hanging Out

A chrysalis hangs from a tree or leaf as the butterfly inside grows. Scientists recreate this structure by pinning pupas to boards at exhibits. A pin is inserted in the silk on top of the chrysalis. If there is no silk to pin, scientists glue a pupa onto a piece of paper and pin the paper to the board.

Staying Separate

Butterflies in exhibits spend their whole lives indoors. How long this life is depends on the butterfly. Monarchs can live as long as eight months. Smaller butterflies only live one week.

Scientists have found that it is a bad idea to release farmed butterflies into the wild. Doing so could hurt wild butterflies. Farmed butterflies could spread deadly diseases to wild butterflies.

Research would also be affected. Scientists carefully collect data about butterflies in the wild. They look at different butterflies' sizes. They also look at where butterflies travel and where they live. Adding farmed butterflies into the wild would give scientists data that is incorrect. This would make it harder to increase the number of wild butterflies being born. That is why it is important to keep farmed butterflies in exhibits their whole lives.

butterfly sticker

TECHNOLOGY

Tag, You're It!

Tagging butterflies is one of the ways scientists learn more about them. When a butterfly is caught and examined, a tiny sticker is placed gently on one wing. Each sticker has a special number. Then, the butterfly is released. If a tagged butterfly is seen, it can be logged online. Scientists can then track where the butterfly travels in its life.

butterfly exhibit

A scientist collects data from a butterfly.

This butterfly has been tagged.

Visiting an Exhibit

Before visiting a butterfly exhibit, it's best to prepare. There are things you can do to make your trip a success. First, find out which types of butterflies are in the exhibit. That way, you will know what you are looking for.

Next, you should know what you would like to do when you visit. Do you want to take pictures or sketch butterflies? If so, you should visit early in the morning or late in the afternoon. That is when butterflies are less active. If you want to watch butterflies in flight, go later in the morning or early in the afternoon.

Finally, think about the clothes you wear. Butterflies are attracted to bright colors. If you wear a brightly colored shirt, they are more likely to land on you. If that doesn't interest you, avoid bright colors.

Students examine a chrysalis in an exhibit.

A butterfly's wing can clearly be seen through the chrysalis.

extreme close-up of a butterfly's head

Butterflies can see color and **ultraviolet** light.

While watching the butterflies in an exhibit, you might notice a butterfly flying back and forth over one area. This behavior is called **patrolling**. It is how a male butterfly looks for a mate.

You might also see a group of butterflies by a water puddle. The puddles have salts and nutrients added to them. Butterflies use the puddles for food.

Since butterflies are cold-blooded, they need a heat source to help warm their bodies. One way butterflies do this is by **basking**. That is when a butterfly uses its wings to get more sun. Usually, one side of a butterfly's wing is darker than the other. The darker areas hold more heat. A butterfly will spread its wings or fold them to point the dark side toward a heat source. In a butterfly exhibit, that heat source may be the sun shining through windows. Or, it may be a lamp that gives off heat.

Butterflies do not sleep, but they do move less at night.

A group of butterflies gathers by a puddle.

A butterfly looks for a mate.

Helping Our Winged Friends

Butterflies need our help. Many butterfly species are **endangered**. They may soon be gone forever. Scientists all over the world have made it their goal to tackle this problem. They have found many ways to help butterflies. But they can't save them alone. One way people can help is by planting milkweed in their gardens. It will attract butterflies and give them places to lay their eggs.

People can also help scientists by keeping track of butterflies in their backyards. They can count how many butterflies they see. They can also take notes on sizes and species. This data can be added to butterfly count websites.

Need more reasons to save butterflies? Visit a butterfly exhibit. You will see hundreds of reasons flying around! Yes, they are beautiful. They are also important to ecosystems and to the future of our world.

There are around 20,000 species of butterflies on Earth.

STEAM CHALLENGE

Define the problem:

Butterflies around the world are losing their habitats. Some people have removed plants that butterflies depend on. One way we can help is by making butterfly feeders. Your task is to design and build a butterfly feeder that will attract local butterflies.

Constraints: You can only use recycled or found items to build your butterfly feeder.

Criteria: Your feeder must have a way to attract butterflies. To appeal to many people, your feeder's height must be adjustable to at least two different heights.

Research and Brainstorm

What do butterflies eat? What are butterflies attracted to? How big should you make your butterfly feeder?

Design and Build

Sketch your design. What about your feeder design will attract butterflies? What materials will work best? Build your feeder.

Test and Improve

Present your design to other students. Explain how it will attract butterflies. Set up your butterfly feeder. Test it by adjusting it to a different height. Does it stay in place? Is it stable? Get feedback. Modify your design and try again.

Reflect and Share

What materials would you use if they did not have to be recycled? What are other ways you could help butterflies? Which part of the process was most challenging?

Glossary

basking—relaxing in a warm place

breeding—mating or producing young plants or animal babies

chrysalis—a hard, protective outer layer of a butterfly pupa; the stage of growth between a caterpillar and a butterfly

climate—the usual weather conditions of a place

compelling—very interesting

ecosystems—the groups of living and nonliving things that make up an environment

endangered—very rare and in danger of dying out completely

extinction—the state of no longer existing

habitats—the areas where plants or animals live

herbicides—chemicals used to destroy plant growth

humid—having a lot of moisture in the air

patrolling—to go around an area for the purpose of watching or protecting

pollinate—to give a plant pollen from another plant

pupas—young insects in the stage between larva and adult

thrive—to develop or grow successfully

ultraviolet—a type of light that humans cannot see

Index

CAREER ADVICE
from Smithsonian

Do you want to work with butterflies?
Here are some tips to get you started.

"There are many plant species that attract butterflies in the Smithsonian's Butterfly Garden. Butterflies feed from nectar plants. They lay eggs on host plants. It is important to learn about plants, gardening, insects, and even chemistry to grow a garden that attracts butterflies."—***James Gagliardi, Horticulturalist***

"I've always loved nature. I studied frogs and insects as a child. I earned a college degree in entomology, the study of insects. A love of nature and insects is very important, as is traveling and exploring. I collect new insect species wherever I go."—***Nate Erwin, Former Manager of the Orkin Insect Zoo and Butterfly Pavilion***